LORD,
HOW CAN
I BLESS
YOU?

A *Fresh* New Approach to your
Relationship with God

Elizabeth Weatherby

WESTBOW
PRESS®
A DIVISION OF THOMAS NELSON
& ZONDERVAN

WestBow Press books may be ordered through booksellers or by contacting:

WestBow Press
A Division of Thomas Nelson & Zondervan
1663 Liberty Drive
Bloomington, IN 47403
www.westbowpress.com
844-714-3454

This was already provided to you. Please add it to the book interior instructions to be added. See project notes.

ISBN: 978-1-9736-8215-8 (sc)
ISBN: 978-1-9736-8214-1 (e)

Print information available on the last page.

WestBow Press rev. date: 11/10/2020

To Jesus Christ,
my Lord, my Best Friend,
who has blessed my life
with this God-opportunity to write
so that I can bless others.

Contents

Part III "Obey Me"

Forward

There are books that inform you, books that entertain you, books that instruct you and books that motivate you. Then there are books that change you. My friend, Elizabeth Weatherby, fondly known as "Libby" to me, has written a book that will change you.

Lord, How Can I Bless You? is the amazing love story between Libby and God. Libby is one of the greatest lovers of God I know. As you read, you'll witness their shared love and how it expands to meet the needs of others. You'll also read of heartbreak, loss, grief, recovery, healing, hope and the miracles of a simple child-like faith. But what you'll witness most is the glory, greatness and wonderment of God.

Lord, How Can I Bless You? is Libby's life story. I've watched her live every word of this book. But Libby doesn't just tell her story; she invites you into it. She's written prayers with each chapter that allow you the opportunity to speak to, hear from and experience the same God she knows and loves. The God she wants you to know loves *you*.

Get ready to laugh, smile and cry. Get ready to be challenged, inspired and convicted. Get ready to fall in love with God and those around you. Get ready to bless God.

If you don't want that kind of reading experience, then don't pick up this book. But if you do, then you're in for the read of your life and more. You're in for a life-change.

Mark Walker, PhD
President, Lee University
Cleveland, TN

Acknowledgments

This book was prophesied by my sweet friend and prayer warrior, Tonia Allen. It was Tonia who believed that I would be the vessel God would use to deliver this on-time message to the body of Christ.

I thank God, too, for my sons, Kells II and Blake, who have loved and believed in their mom and who are my strongest supporters. To my sweet daughters-in-love, Shannon and Krystin, thank you for your encouragement. I love you dearly. And to Grandma's delight, Kells III, Isaac, Nora Grace, Olivia, Lincoln, Maddox and Kai, you are my inspiration.

Mary Meadows, my sister-in-love, how I appreciate you for your many years of faithful prayer and the seed you have sown into this ministry to help me accomplish the mission God has given me. I could not have done it without you! Thank you for obeying when the Spirit of God leads you to pray and to give.

Gay Henry, my longtime friend and sister in Christ, you have partnered with me in so many ways to get this message out. I thank God for your friendship.

Ann Platz, woman of love and compassion, you encouraged me to make divine connections and you continue to inspire and mentor me.

Pastor Mark Walker, PhD, the Lord blessed me by placing me under your covering. Thank you so very much for your love, prayers and support.

Dianna Douglass, you took years of my spiritual diaries, read my heart and put it on paper to produce a workable manuscript. Thank you!

Anne Severance, my editor, you were God's chosen for my first book, and I praise Him for your tender, loving heart, for your patience and for believing in me. I love you.

Don and Chris Wise, my publishing support, what a glorious team! You have made this first publishing venture fun and creative, one that has resulted in an enduring friendship. I love you both! Your servant hearts are so appreciated. I also want to thank God for my Pastor, Gloria Gainor, for her love, prayers and support.

Introduction

Hello, precious new friends,

I am so excited to share the deepest part of my heart with you in this book, born after years of journaling my thoughts and questions to the Lord and hearing His answers to me. I have never written a book before, but I do know that God has asked me to deliver a very important message – with your name on it.

Sitting at my desk one day, I felt the Lord saying, *I have a message for My people and you are the messenger.* What an honor to be chosen to speak for the Lord.

It all began in 1985 when I got down on my knees and admitted that I had made a mess of my life. I was tired of doing things my way and surrendered my will to Jesus Christ, making Him my Lord and Savior. That's also when I started a crash course in *Blessings 101.* I soon learned that the God of the Universe, who loves us so much that He didn't withhold anything – not even His only Son, Jesus Christ – absolutely delights in giving good gifts to His children

My gratitude for His amazing love has grown by leaps and bounds. Right before my eyes, God has proven His love for me in so many tangible ways. He gives me my daily bread (often literally), the gift of a car (out of the blue!) when I had no transportation, and, most exciting of all, support for a ministry the Lord called me to found: *Feed My Lambs* - a grassroots, nonprofit organization that opened Christian schools for some of the poorest children in the United States, Africa and Mexico.

In this self-centered age we live in, when so many of us are seeking material possessions and pleasure more than God, I felt led to ask, "Lord, how can I bless you?" I heard God Say:

Love Me, Trust Me, Obey Me.

At that moment I knew that this was the message He wanted me to share. To make it easy for you to hear my heart, this book is divided into the three "words" God spoke to me. Under each section are stories about His mighty hand of mercy and grace, powerful Scriptures that have guided my faith-walk, a prayer that you may want to pray along with me and a "God nugget" that He has dropped into my life. The testimonies are not necessarily in the order in which they happened, because this book is not about me. It is a book about God's faithfulness.

My heart's desire is that this book will bless you and bring you to the place where Jesus Christ is your First Love, and that you, too, will wake up each morning, asking, "Lord, how can I bless You?"

PART 1
"LOVE ME"

Jesus said,
"You shall love the Lord your God
with all your heart,
with all your soul,
and with all your mind."
This is the first and greatest
commandment,
and the second is like it:
"you shall love your neighbor as
yourself."

- Matthew 22:37 – 39

1

Baby Dolls and Daydreams

Unless you are converted and become as little children,
you will by no means enter the kingdom of heaven.

--Matthew 18:3

Although my parents were divorced, as a little child I always felt
love all around me. Maybe that was partly because I looked like
my mother, with blonde hair and huge blue eyes. Or maybe it was
to make up for the fact that I lived in a "broken" home. Although
my Momma and Daddy are now deceased, all I knew as a child
was that Momma loved me and Daddy loved me (even if he wasn't
living with us anymore), and I loved them too.

For me, back then, love meant hugs and cuddles, baby dolls
and daydreams, and feeling the admiration of those around me.
Like when Daddy took me to a truck stop and asked me to sing
and dance for the truckers. I loved to sing and I loved people, so it
just seemed the natural thing to do. At other times, he made and
hauled "white lightin" through the mountains of North Georgia.
He would set me on top of the boxes of liquor and I'd wave and
smile at the policeman in their patrol cars as they passed by.

Granny (now deceased) once told me that my daddy was "called of God" to preach, but he loved alcohol more.

All of which caused me, a little later on, to wonder what love was all about. If I loved dolls and Daddy loved whiskey and Momma loved me – what did love really mean anyway?

After the divorce, my momma moved my brother, sister and me into a government housing home. When a local church sent a bus to pick us up for Sunday school and Bible camp, I began to learn about another kind of love – *agape* – God's love. This love doesn't look at the outside. It doesn't care about your hair color or your skin color or where you live. It's a giving kind of love. And when I heard that God gave His only Son to die for our sins, I knew I wanted Jesus to come live in my heart. I didn't understand at the time that I was also to let go of my own selfish desires and make Him the Lord of my life.

God asks for childlike faith. It is with childlike faith that I go to the Lord, and it is childlike faith that helps me to see myself sitting in my heavenly Father's lap, letting Him love me and loving Him back. In my travels throughout the United States and other countries, I see so many people who try to fill the emptiness in their hearts with drugs, alcohol, sex or material possessions. What they are really looking for is love. They just don't know that His name is Jesus.

Now, each morning when I wake up, I tell my Heavenly Father how much I love Him and that I desire to bless Him and worship Him this day with my life as well as to be a blessing to others. With childlike anticipation, I ask, "Lord, how can *I* bless *You?*"

Are you ready to take your eyes off yourself and focus on Him? If you will begin today praying this prayer with me, by the end of one month, you will have a brand-new mindset toward the One who knows you best and loves you most. God will open up new doors and windows of opportunity that you could never have imagined in all your wildest dreams.

Prayer: *Dear Heavenly Father, thank you for loving me. You're such a kind and merciful Father. You care about everything that happens to me. I know I am safe in Your lap, close to Your heart. I desire to bless You by loving You, trusting You and obeying You every moment of every day. In Jesus' name, amen.*

2

Satin, Lace and Love

For your Maker is your husband – the Lord Almighty is His name.

--Isaiah 54:5

The year was 1972. He was good looking, with long, curly sandy-blond hair and gorgeous blue eyes…Oh, but I'm getting ahead of myself! Let's back up.

My roommate and I, who worked together at the local Waffle House, had just returned from training in Texas. When we got home, my roommate's sister and her friend wanted us to take them to see their boyfriends who played in a band. The four of us drank Cokes and danced the night away. By the end of the evening, the waitress was bringing me Cokes without charging me. Apparently, the owner (now deceased) had a son named Kells Weatherby and he had picked up my tab.

Later that month, when all my friends and I returned to the club, Kells asked me for a date to Victoria Station Restaurant. He came to my door with a bouquet of beautiful flowers, a bottle of wine and a newspaper with all the movie listings. I was blown away! About halfway through our delicious meal, Kells looked over at me, leaned back in his chair and said, "How would you like to be Elizabeth *Weatherby?*"

I was shocked. "Aren't we moving a little too fast? This is only our first date."

"I know what I want and it's *you*. My hunt is over."

From that first date on, the two of us were never apart, and six months later we were married. When you fall in love with someone, you can't wait to be together. You want to look good, smell good, sound good. You feel so happy when you are around each other that you don't want to let him/her out of your sight. You just want to love each other, serve each other, give to each other, talk to each other, laugh and cry together. You delight in every little thing about the one you love.

At the time Kells and I were married, Jesus was not the Lord of our lives. It wasn't until fifteen years later that we truly learned to love each other God's way – by making Jesus our First Love.

After thirty-two years of marriage, Kells went Home to be with Jesus. I was so happy for him, but after spending all those years together, I missed him terribly.

As I was browsing through a store the other day, I saw a long satin, lace and pearl nightgown. It was so beautiful it took my breathe away. As I stopped to look at it, tears welled up in my eyes. I thought to myself, *Elizabeth, what are you doing? You don't need a beautiful gown like this! Kells is gone.*

All of a sudden I heard in my heart a soft, sweet voice saying, *I am your Husband now.* I began to cry. I knew that was the Holy Spirit of God speaking to me. I bought the gown that day and decided to wear it for my Lord who is my First Love.

Is the Lord *your* First Love? I'm so excited about Jesus that I want to please Him, to love Him, to trust and obey Him. I care what He thinks about me, about the places I go, even about what I wear! He fills my heart with His love, joy and peace.

It is so awesome to do God's work, to love on His people and to help those in need. But I must not forget to spend time with

Him. Like those early romantic days when I first fell in love with Kells, Jesus wants me to sit with Him, read His love letters (His Holy Word), pray to Him, walk with Him, sing to Him, thank Him and praise Him in all things. May I encourage you to follow Jesus Christ and be filled daily with God's Holy Spirit, who will teach you amazing secrets about living a love-filled life.

Prayer: *Abba Father, I love You. I invite You into every room of my heart. You are my delight! I love to be with You. I can't bear to be separated from You – through sin or selfishness. You, O Lord, are my desire. I want so much to bless You, to love You, to worship You with my life. As I do this, I am able by Your love and grace to love and serve others. In Jesus' name, amen.*

3

Submission Is Not
a Dirty Word

Submit to one another in the fear of the Lord.

-- Ephesians 5:21

The first fifteen years of our marriage, Kells and I attended church, gave our tithe when it was convenient and occasionally read our Bibles. To tell you the truth, even though both of us loved Jesus, we did not allow Him to lead us. Although we were saved during our childhood years, neither of us ever really made Jesus the Lord of our lives until much later. Of course, we always wanted Him to bless us, including our lifestyle, our stuff and everything we wanted to do.

The last seventeen years of our marriage, however, were much different. By this time, we had surrendered ourselves to Jesus, giving our hearts totally to God. Were we perfect after that? No, but our priorities had definitely changed. As Kells liked to say, "Put God first, spouse second, family third, then church, followed by job – in that order."

The most radical step I took was repenting for all the wrong decisions I had made and refusing to blame others for them. In 1985, I felt like my life was falling apart and that I had made a mess of things. I got out of bed, knelt down and cried out to God to forgive me for going my own way and doing my own thing. That had only gotten me into big trouble. This time I desired God's perfect will for my life – to submit, surrender and follow Jesus.

The very next day, I was sitting in church and God's Presence came upon me so strongly that my life has never been the same! Even our marriage changed.

The more consistently we followed Jesus – loving and serving Him – the more deeply we fell in love with each other. I began reading in God's Word about His views on marriage and how to love, serve and submit to my husband as unto the Lord. I must admit, it was a tough lesson. For fifteen years, Kells had given, given, given and I had taken, taken, taken. Oh, he had his faults too. In fact, we both served our own selfish selves for almost half our married lives.

But, praise God, we found that to be truly happy and fulfilled, our love for God had to come first. If we had not made Jesus the Lord of our lives and the Head of our home, I don't believe Kells and I would have made it, and our marriage would have become just another ugly statistic. By God's grace and because we submitted to His plan we learned to love, serve and honor each other.

To stop blaming others for the wrong decisions I have made is one of the best lessons I have ever learned in my life. My prayer for you is that you don't have to wait as long as I did.

Prayer: *Heavenly Father, thank You for teaching my husband and me how to love You first, then each other. I am so grateful that You gave us some good years to practice our new love walk before You took my husband Home to be with You. I love You, Lord. In Jesus' name, amen.*

4

On Top of the World

If anyone desires to come after Me, let him deny himself, and take up his cross and follow me.

—Matthew 16:24

I have always loved music. Before I became a Christian, I went to Nashville to record my very first record, "She'll Have to Go through Me to Get to You." While I was in the studio, my producer would say to me, "Put your heart into it, Libby."

Everywhere I went, people loved to hear me sing with my Patsy Cline twang. I had the opportunity to perform at Gilley's in Texas, at the MGM in Las Vegas and the Steeplechase in Atlanta, Georgia. I would be lying to you if I told you it wasn't fun, because it was.

It was about time for my record to be released in the Southeastern region of the U.S. and I was getting so excited. After the record came out, I knew that I would be singing even more. I couldn't wait!

Not only did I have a record deal, but my husband and I worked for a businessman in Atlanta who owed several companies. I was a top salesperson for one of his companies, and Kells managed another. We made great money, had a new home, two cars and traveled whenever we liked. We weren't rich, but we enjoyed a comfortable lifestyle. Kells and I were just going along our self-centered way, looking good and keeping up with the Joneses.

Then one day, suddenly, it felt as if a rug had been pulled out from under us. We lost everything: our jobs, our home, our stock, even our Mercedes. Our life sounded almost like a country song, but this was no song lyric. It was reality. It happened to us overnight – from sitting on top of the world to scraping ourselves off the ground at the bottom of the ladder.

The IRS had come in and locked the doors to our boss's companies without any warning. You see, at this time our trust was in jobs, paychecks and people.

Now you have to remember, we loved the Lord, we went to church sometimes and we threw a little money in the collection bucket whenever we felt like it. As a matter of fact, we thought we were living a great life. Then when we lost all our possessions, everything changed. Our marriage suffered, and we almost lost that, too, due to this horrible trial…at least that's what I thought at the time.

If you asked me today, though, I would say, "Thank You, God, for loving us too much to leave us where we were." Our trial turned out to be a victory for our family. God is so good and faithful. I am not saying that we lived a perfect life after this, but I am speaking of a decision Kells and I made to surrender everything to follow Jesus.

With that, I was ready to go to the next level with Jesus and really "put my heart into it," as my record producer had previously told me. I felt led to cancel my recording contract and said to the Lord, "Now I can sing for *You*."

Deep within my heart, the Spirit of God said, *You don't know Me.*

He was right. I didn't really know the Lord very well. That's when I decided to take a three-year course at a Bible college in the

Metro Atlanta area to learn more about God. While I was still in school, He began opening doors for me to sing in churches and prisons. This time, I would be singing and preaching about His love ... and I couldn't wait!

Prayer: *Heavenly Father, forgive me for my foolish choices. Help me not to love the things of this world, but to love and follow You. Please give me the opportunity to love and give to others as You have loved and forgiven me. My heart's desire is to sing Your praises forever. I love You, Lord. In Jesus' name, amen.*

5

A Little Bit of Heaven

They will know you are My disciples if you have love for one another.

-- John 13:35

I was ministering in a women's day shelter, hoping to start a Bible study for the ladies. On fire for God, I was ready – or at least I *thought* I was ready. But I soon found that most of the ladies had not the slightest interest in sitting down to hear my thoughts on the Word of God. Week after week, I would return with my Bible, to no avail.

Then one day I heard God speak to me: *Elizabeth, what are you doing?*

"I'm just doing what You told me to do, Lord," I replied, a little surprised that He would ask, "but they don't want to hear it."

By His Holy Spirit, I felt God speak softly to my heart: *No, Elizabeth. What I told you to do was to go love on the ladies and listen to them. Then they will listen to My Word.*

After that, I did exactly as God had told me, allowing His Spirit to guide me and fill me with His love for these precious women.

As some of them began to tell me about their lives, they began releasing their pent-up rage and anger. I could see that the women were hurt, angry and wounded. I so wanted to show them the love of Jesus as I simply sat on the floor, listened to them, and played with their children. Before long, I was hugging and kissing everybody, whether they wanted me to or not. Still, I was disappointed that I couldn't teach them about the Bible.

One day after leaving the shelter, I got into my van, leaned my head against the steering wheel and began to cry. One of the ladies from the shelter saw me and started walking over to me.

As I rolled down the window, I heard her sweet, pleading voice, "Ms. Libby, we've been watching you to see if you really love us. Some women just come down here to the shelter, drop off their bags of clothes and feel like they've done their 'good deed' for the year. They don't seem to really care about *us*. But Ms. Libby, you're different. Don't leave us. We can see your love for us."

Then I *really* started crying, knowing God was speaking straight to my heart. What a wonderful lesson. God was looking for my willingness so He could use me to love and serve others.

How can the world see Jesus if we don't demonstrate His love? That day at the shelter, I learned that they have to see His love in *us* before they can believe in *Him*. Jesus said, "By this all will know that you are My disciples, if you have love for one another" (John 13:35)

I dried my tears, thanked the woman for encouraging *me* and gave her a hug. "I'll be back, I promise."

Prayer: *Lord, I want to thank you for the opportunities You give me everyday to love and serve others. Please open my ears to be able to hear Your voice and respond to Your plan. Open my eyes so that I can see the needs around me and bless others in order to bless You. I love You. In Jesus' name, amen.*

6

One Miracle After Another

Eye has not seen, nor ear heard, nor have entered into the heart of man the things which God has prepared for those who love Him.

--1 Corinthians 2:9

Do you believe in miracles? I certainly do! In the early 90's, I was invited to speak and sing in a small church off Moore's Mill Road in Atlanta. The people there were warm and friendly, such a blessing.

After the service, my husband and I drove to Kroger. While I waited for Kells to pick up something for our lunch, I opened my Bible and was surprised to find a beautiful, cream-colored envelope edged in gold. Inside was a note that read: "I am the God who supplies all your need. I own the cattle on a thousand hills. That's why your truck is paid in full. I love you." The note was signed simple: "J".

Enclosed was a bill from the bank marked "Paid in Full." It was the note for $2,000 that my husband still owed on his Ford truck. That little gray truck was the only transportation our family had for a while, and there were lots of happy memories associated with it. We would drive to Gadsden, Alabama, to see Grandma, and Kells II and I would lie in the back under a blue tarp when it rained. What fun!

But who in the world would have paid off the note for us? I didn't know anyone who might have slipped the envelope into my Bible, but it must have been someone from the church. Kells wanted to know why I was crying when he came back to the van. When I explained, he practically shouted, "Praise God!" I noticed the tears in *his* eyes too.

The next day Kells stopped by the bank, but we were never able to find out who had paid off that loan. We decided that the note was from our Lord Jesus, and however He had chosen to pay it was between Him and that person.

Another time I was praying with Gay, my prayer partner, in her beautiful home. We prayed for our children, and as I was getting ready to leave, she said, "Wait a minute...I have something for you." She proceeded to load up my van with gourmet food – steaks, fish, wonderful items that I would never have bought for myself. Little did my friend know that we had no groceries in all the house that day. But God knew! And He showered us with love gifts.

You need to know that nothing was said to any of these people about our needs. My family and I had not asked for anything. We simply go out and share the gospel of Jesus Christ because of our love and commitment to Him, and He blesses us. I enjoy going into my prayer closet and talking to God about everything and every need in my life. After falling in love with my Lord, trusting Him in everything is a safe place for me.

Do you need a miracle today? God loves to bless His children, and He is just waiting to bless *you*. He's full of wonderful surprises!

Prayer: *Heavenly Father, thank You for all the miracles that You have given to my family. But the greatest miracle You have given to us is Jesus Christ, Your Son. How delightful it is to serve such an awesome God. I love you so very much. In Jesus' name, amen.*

7

My Love Walk with Jesus

Every day I will bless You, and I will praise Your name for ever and ever.

--Psalm 145:2

Early in the morning…birds chirping…my workout clothes on… then out the door. I'm ready for my walk - my walk with Jesus. It's my favorite time to talk with Him.

As I begin my morning walk, I take a deep breath, look up toward heaven and begin to praise God. "Good morning, Father. I love You with all my heart, all my soul, all my mind and all my strength. Thank You for this beautiful morning. Thank You, Lord, that You have already provided my every need this very day. And now, Lord, how can I bless you?"

I love this time with my Lord. I take my prayer book, and begin to decree God's promises over those I love – my family, friends and covenant partners – and the lost and hurting. As I begin to pray, I ask that "[each of us] may be filled with the knowledge of His will in all wisdom and spiritual understanding; that you may have a walk worthy of the Lord, fully pleasing Him, being fruitful in every good work and increasing in the knowledge of God" (Col. 1: 9,10)

Praying the Scriptures back to the Father encourages my heart and blesses Him. As Jesus Himself said, "If you abide in Me, and My words abide in you, you will ask what you desire, and it shall be done for you" (John 15:7).

But there is more to "walking with Jesus" than an early-morning jog. When we choose to walk in love toward others – love, faithfulness and self-control – we are walking with Him. In my own strength, I could not get very far on this journey, but through Jesus Christ, I can do all things (see Phil 4:13). My friends, you will never be the same if you decide to start your day with Jesus, telling Him that you love Him, trust Him for the day and desire to obey Him.

Prayer: *Lord, I love You. I truly desire to give You everything today – every thought, every word, every action, every attitude. I need You, Lord. Help me to walk out this day and the rest of my life with You. Thank You for reminding me that You are with me wherever I go. In Jesus' name, amen.*

8

Big Red Bow

My God shall supply all your need according to His riches in glory by Christ Jesus.

-- Philippians 4:19

Fall was upon us and it was time to begin preparing for the new school year. Our two boys, Kells II and Blake, needed school clothes. At that time, their dad's construction business was in a slump, and I was just starting out in ministry. Money was tight.

Before bedtime one night, I gathered the boys for prayer and we held hands. I said to Kells II, "You pray and I'll agree with you. God will hear your prayer and answer it."

Kells II began to pray, "Jesus, me and Blake need some school clothes. Can You help my dad with a job so we can get the stuff we need? Amen." Both boys went to bed.

Friday night of that same week, my precious friend Gay picked me up and drove me to a women's conference. After the conference was over, she brought me home. As she rolled up to the house, she popped the trunk of her car and pulled out several bags of clothes.

"What is all this?" I asked.

Gay told me she had been shopping for her daughter at the Gap, which happened to be our sons' favorite store. The Lord had told her to buy clothes for Kells II and Blake. As I stood there, I began to cry. At that moment, I knew that God had heard the boys' prayers.

God is so faithful. The next morning, when the boys woke up, they found the school clothes we had prayed and believed for. They were so excited! We had thought that God was going to bless their dad with a job to buy the clothes, but He had another plan.

Saints, we must learn that God works through His people to bless one another. My sweet friend loved the Lord enough to hear His voice and was obedient to follow through. Gay was doing exactly what the Word tells us to do: Love one another by clothing and feeding those in need (See Matt. 25:35-40).

But that's not the end of the story. That Saturday morning, I had the opportunity to speak and sing at a Women's Aglow meeting. I had picked out my outfit – a black skirt and a red jacket. My hair was long at that time, so I wanted to pull it back with a bow.

Earlier that week, I had gone over to visit my niece Christy at her home and had noticed a black hair bow on her dresser. (I really wanted a red bow to match my jacket, but the black one would do just fine). When I went to ask Christy if I could borrow her hair bow, I heard the Lord tell me to put it back. *I will provide*, He promised.

That's all I heard. So I obeyed. Why? Because I love God so much. Even though my niece offered to lend me the bow, I refused, explaining, "I believe God has another plan."

As I was getting dressed on Saturday morning, I looked over at the bags of clothes Gay had bought the boys. When I saw a big red bow on top of one of the bags, I knew that God had kept His promise! Later, Gay shared with me that the Lord had told her to buy the bow for me as she was leaving the Gap.

We never have to doubt God's love for us. He designed us in His image and then provides the perfect accessories. I shared my "red bow" testimony with the ladies that morning. There wasn't a dry eye in the room. Even in the smallest details of my life, God always desires to bless His children. To God be the glory!

Prayer: *Heavenly Father, help me never to forget Your love for each of us. You hear our every prayer and answer in Your own special way. We are so blessed to be Your children. I love You, Lord. In the precious name of Jesus, amen.*

9

Family Alert

Whoever receives one little child like this in My name
receives Me.

--Matthew 18:5

When I began to minister at the women and children's shelters in Atlanta, Georgia, in the late '80s and early '90s, I met a precious little blond-haired, blue-eyed girl. She was living in the night shelter with her mother, who was pregnant, and her younger brother and sister. She was not happy there and wanted her own home and her own bed.

After visiting the shelter on a regular basis, her mother allowed me to take her home with me on the weekends. She went lots of places with us, just like she was part of our family. Our boys even enjoyed having her in our home.

One day I got a phone call from the Atlanta night shelter. It was her mom who was going into labor. I immediately got in my car and drove to the shelter to pick up the mom and take her to the hospital. A few hours later, a beautiful little girl was born.

My husband and I hated to see this little family go back to the shelter to live, so we helped the mother move into an apartment, helped her get furniture, bedding and food. She was so thankful, and the children were much happier too. For a while, everything went well, then something happened and the family lost their apartment and was homeless again.

This time we went to the Housing Authority and God gave us favor. After we got this precious family settled into another new home, I decided to drop by for an unexpected visit. The mom was on the couch, some of the children were lying on the floor watching TV, and one was was trying to take care of the baby. I went over to pick up the baby. The smell was unbearable. I thought she had a dirty diaper, but I could tell that the baby had not been bathed in quite some time, and she had a bad cold.

I was saddened to see a newborn baby in that condition, so I asked her mom if I could take the children home with me for the weekend. Of course she said yes. My family and I so enjoyed the children. By Sunday afternoon, after a wonderful weekend, it was time to take them home.

When we arrived at the house, no one was there. We asked the neighbors, but none of them had any idea where the mom was. We took the children back home and kept them for several weeks. Through the Department of Family and Children's Services, we learned that the mother was still collecting a check from the government. They tracked her down and found her living in undesirable conditions not far from her old apartment. Since we had found the mom, by law we had to return the children to her, which we did.

At a later meeting with the mother she grabbed me and cried, "Ms. Libby I love you! You and Mr. Kells have been so good to my children and me."

I was so thankful to God for His mercy and love. The end result was that the mom was not able to keep her children but all are in loving homes.

That little blond-haired, blue-eyed girl is all grown up now.

I am so glad that God used us to pour His love over this little family. I pray that you will be listening for "alerts" in your life.

Prayer: *Help me to remember, Lord, that love always forgives, love always serves and love always wins. Please bless and protect the little children. In Jesus' name, amen.*

10

The Voice

I know your works. See, I have set before you an open door, And no one can shut it; for you have a little strength, have kept My Word, and have not denied My name.

-- Revelation 3:8

The voice of the Lord came to me very clearly one day: *You shall open Christian schools in poverty areas.* Later on, I heard: *Go get the babies and the little children.*

When God spoke to me, I knew it was His voice I had heard and not my own. At that time, I was living in Houston, Texas. I was a wife and mother of two sons, working in the corporate world. My prayer life in those days was limited to asking God what *He* could do for *me.* Since nothing like this had ever happened before, I was certainly not expecting God to ask *me* to do something for *Him.*

The thought had never entered my mind that I would open Christian schools for poor children. When God spoke to me, I did not understand what it meant or how I was going to do it. I just knew it was God.

His call never comes at a "convenient time" and we are usually not qualified (in the world's eye) for the task. I was not a schoolteacher, nor did I have a degree in education, which would be the obvious credentials to start up any kind of school. I do love people and have always been willing to help anyone, but my focus was more on myself, my family and friends – not the poor.

When I heard God's voice, it was loud and strong, yet gentle. He did not ask me – it was more like a mandate. In retrospect, I believe God knew I would surrender all and obey Him. A couple of years later, that's exactly what I did. I gave it all up – all my stuff – along with my ambitions, my desires and my dreams so that I could follow the Lord Jesus Christ. I remember telling Him, "Lord, from now on, You choose where I live, what I drive and what I wear. I don't have time to seek after those things. I'm just going to seek You, and love and serve others."

I am so thankful that God called me, anointed me and sent me out to love on His people and to "go get the babies." My heart yielded to Him, as He sent me to the inner city to found our ministry.

This was the beginning of a long and beautiful journey that God had planned. To be honest, I was a little shaky at first and my priorities had to change. God was calling our entire family to be surrendered to Him. He had a work, a purpose and a plan for each of us, just as He has a purpose and a plan for you.

When you hear God's voice and discover His purpose for your life, don't let anything stop you until you fulfill it!

Prayer: *Lord, please help us to listen for Your still, small voice. Give us the grace and the strength to live exactly as You have commanded: first, loving You with all our hearts, all our souls and all our minds; then, loving our neighbors as ourselves. Encourage us to walk through the open doors You provide for those who keep Your Word and do not deny Your name. I love You. In the precious name of Jesus, amen.*

PART II
"TRUST ME"

Blessed is the man who trusts in the Lord,
Whose trust is the Lord.

-- Jeremiah 17:7 (ESV)

11

Level Four Faith

*I sought the Lord and He heard me and delivered me
from all my fears.*

-- Psalm 34:4

"How long have you had that little black mole?" My friend Nancy
wanted to know one day while we were on a mission trip to
Mexico.

I glanced down to see what she was talking about. The small
mole on my stomach seemed pretty harmless to me. "Oh, I don't
know. About two years, I guess."

"Well, you are going to have to see my dermatologist in
Atlanta when we get back home!"

Nancy followed through on her promise as soon as she could
schedule an appointment for me. The doctor biopsied the mole
and sent it off to be tested.

In the meantime, I was too busy with my children's work to
think much about it. When I had a spare minute or two, I did
wonder about some strange symptoms I had noticed in the past
few months. My left leg would swell, my nails were breaking and
my hair seemed to be getting thinner.

About a month later, my husband Kells and I were on our way to West Virginia, taking school supplies, food and clothes to some needy children there. Ever since we had discovered our new mission in life – opening Christian schools for children in poverty-stricken areas – we had never been happier.

We were discussing this when Kell's cell phone rang. It was my doctor. Although I couldn't hear what she was saying, I could see the worried expression on my husband's face. He handed the phone to me.

"Elizabeth," said the doctor, "I'm afraid I have some bad news for you. You must come back to Atlanta immediately. The biopsy report is in and the mole was melanoma. Level four. It's very serious, but we'll get the best surgeon at Emory University Hospital."

I guess you could say I was in shock, trying to take it all in. I told my doctor that I couldn't come until we had completed our mission trip to West Virginia. After hanging up the phone, Kells grabbed my hand and pulled me close to him. He really didn't say much. He didn't have to. He was just loving on me, which is what I really needed.

All of a sudden, I heard a voice speaking clearing to my heart. *Do you believe what you preach?*

The next morning my friend Kelly and I were looking for a Scripture when I felt led to read Psalm 34:4: "I sought the Lord and He heard me, and delivered me from all my fears." I knew in my heart that God was speaking to me through His Word. The moment I decided to trust God for the outcome, all fear left me and such a peace swept over my heart and mind.

I would not tell relatives and friends about the trial I was going through unless they were born-again believers who had faith in God to stand with me during this time. I did not want negative words and death spoken over me, only words of life, blessing and truth.

We must be careful whom we ask to pray for us. When people

tell me they are praying for me, I am always grateful, but I ask them to speak only what God's Word says about the situation. Scriptures such as Isaiah 53:5 meant the world to me: "He was bruised for our iniquities; the chastisement for our peace was upon Him [Jesus] and by His stripes we are healed." I clung to this and other passages during this difficult time.

I agreed to the surgery, and my husband and I were introduced to Dr. Douglas R. Murray of Emory University Hospital. He was absolutely wonderful and so compassionate. A young lady, Susan, also helped me prepare for the surgery, and I was able to share my faith in Jesus Christ with her. We are still friends today.

"There is no cancer." Those were the first words I heard in the recovery room as I began to wake up from the anesthesia.

I thank my Lord every day for His divine health! I tell myself, as I am telling you now: Never take anything for granted, always have a grateful heart and let God know every day how thankful you are.

Prayer: *Thank You, Lord, for sparing my life. Thank You that I can see, hear, walk and talk. May I never take for granted Your glorious gifts – life, health, family, friends, finances. You are so good and I am so grateful that you are my love and my joy. In the name of my precious Jesus, amen.*

12

Bad Hair Day!

Whoever trusts in the Lord, happy is he.

--Proverbs 15:20b

In the midst of a busy schedule working in the ministry, God opened doors for me that no man could shut.

One of those doors was TBN, a Christian network, which had heard about Feed My Lambs and wanted to interview me. Since it would be my first time to appear on television, I asked my husband if he had the money for me to get my hair done.

"Not now, I don't," Kells said, "but we'll believe God for it." So, by faith, I made an appointment at a local salon.

When the day came for the television appearance, I called my husband. "It's time to go get my hair done. Do we have the money yet?"

"No," he replied sadly. "I'm sorry, baby, we don't."

I hung up the phone, feeling a little discouraged. My hair was a mess and I really wanted it to look great for the taping.

Suddenly I heard a voice telling me to go on to the salon. *I will provide.*

"Is that You, God?" I aked out loud. "Are You talking to me?"

You see, I love God, I trust Him and desire to obey Him. I also know that He loves me and hears my heart's desire.

I drove to the salon, not knowing how God was going to provide, but completely trusting Him to do it. In the back of my mind, I was thinking, *God is going to tell the hairdresser to give me a blessing.*

Unsure of what the Lord was about to do, I stepped out on faith and put feet to my prayer. I pulled up to the salon, parked and got out of the van. At that moment, I felt a breeze brush my ankles and I looked down. There, on the ground at my feet, was a twenty-dollar bill, which in the early '90s would have covered everything I needed to have done that day. Praise God! He is so faithful!

I marched right into the salon with my money as if I had had it all along. You see, God wants us to *ask* in faith and *act* in faith as if what we are asking is already a fact. God is looking for people like you and me to do great and mighty things. He is looking for loyal hearts. He is especially pleased with childlike faith. He wants us to depend upon Him and not upon our own ability to figure things out. God knows us, loves us and wants to bless His children. Sometimes, we as Christians must get *up* and do something – act in faith – and not just sit back and wait.

My heart's desire is that this testimony of God's faithfulness is a blessing to you and will help to increase your faith in Him. No matter what situation you are facing today, God has already made a way for you. "Thanks be to God, who gives us the victory through our Lord Jesus Christ" (1 Cor. 15:57)

Prayer: *Thank You, Lord, that Your eyes are searching the whole earth for people who have committed their lives completely to You. Give us the faith, even in the little things, to trust You completely to answer in any way You choose. I love You, Lord. In Jesus' name, amen.*

13

The Burgundy Bread Van

*And whatever we ask we receive from Him, because
we keep His commandments and do those things that
are pleasing in His sight.*

--1 John 3:22

Early in my ministry, while I was preaching and singing in jails
and youth detention centers, and working in women's shelters, I
felt in my heart that God also wanted me to go and feed the poor.
We had one small Ford pickup and my husband needed it for his
job, so I guess you could say we had to share.

I began talking to God about our family needing another
vehicle. One day, while I was alone in our two-bedroom
apartment – just the cat, the dog and me – the phone rang. The
caller was a woman named Mary, whom I had never met. "Hello?
Is this the ministry that needs a van?"

"Yes, ma'am," I replied, my heart beating fast. "I have been
trusting God for a van so I can deliver food to the poor. But how
did you know?"

She told me that she had gone to the office of the *Thrifty*

Nickel to place an advertisement. While there, she noticed a very short ad in the paper on the counter.

I knew *I* had not put the ad in the paper. It must have been my precious friend Donna, who owned the local *Thrifty Nickel* at that time. Donna loves God and always listens when He speaks. She later confessed that she had placed the ad for me. I'm sure God moved on her heart to do that.

After Mary and I talked a little more about our ministry, she asked me where I did my banking. When I told her, she said she would meet me there the following week with the new Volkswagen van as a donation to the ministry. Mary said to me, "I bought this van in Alabama six months ago and didn't really know why." All I could say was, "Praise God! I love you, Lord! Thank you, Lord!" When I hung up after our conversation, I began shouting so loud my pets went crazy. Praise God, He had answered my prayer – six months before I had prayed it!

When I met Mary at the bank the next week, she had a beautiful burgundy van for me – with only a thousand miles on it. It still looked brand new, with plastic over the seats and plush carpet. She gave me the title, the keys and a great big hug. We prayed together, thanking God for His provision and asking Him to bless Mary for her unselfish gift.

Soon afterward, I began picking up fruit, bread and sweets from grocery stores in the metro Atlanta area. Seven days a week, I delivered these items to the needy. I was like a butterfly on wheels. I drove everywhere, even into the poorest neighborhoods, where there were constant shootings, drugs and alcohol abuse. As long as I knew Jesus had called me, I felt safe.

That van also carried donated Bibles into government housing homes, mobile home parks, and shelters, where I began to hold Bible studies. I took food to the teenagers in a drug rehab. The kids there called me "The Church Lady." When I was asked to teach the Word of God every Sunday night, I said yes right away and continued teaching for years. Others joined me from the body of Christ to serve and minister, and many souls were saved, healed and delivered through the bread ministry.

Since then, other individuals and churches have responded with additional vehicles to assist in this ministry. I thank God that He has chosen me to serve, but He has also chosen you. If we pray, sincerely asking for His direction, He will answer. He blesses us to be a blessing to others. You just have to be available to Him…God will do the rest.

Prayers: *Dear God, may we never take anyone or anything for granted. Thank you that, according to 2 Chronicles 16:9, "The eyes of the LORD run to and fro throughout the whole earth, to show Himself strong on behalf of those whose heart is loyal to Him." Thank you for doing great and mighty things through "listeners" like Mary. It is a joy to give, but it is also a blessing to receive answers to our prayers. I love You, Lord. In Jesus' name, amen.*

14

Be Careful What You Say

Train up a child in the way he should go, And when he is old he will not depart from it.

--Proverbs 22:6

I was so mad at my teenage son Kells for being disrespectful and talking back to me. What an attitude! The truth of the matter was that he had a rebellious heart toward God, his parents and anyone in authority. He had been attending a Christian school since the fourth grade, and he knew better than that.

Even the teachers recognized this boy's strong leadership potential, but they were very concerned about some of the decisions he was making. He knew the Word of God as well as his dad and I and sometimes even challenged the Bible teacher in class. But somewhere along the way, he had taken a wrong turn.

It all started when a new student enrolled in my son's school, and the two boys started to hang out together. Before long my son decided to stop playing sports even though he was one of the top players and a favorite of the coaches.

After that, things went from bad to worse. He began making

choices contrary to the way he was taught and raised. As a mom, I went into denial. Not *my* son! He would never do *that!*

To make matters worse, I interfered with my wise husband's attempts to correct him. I couldn't see that the Lord was at work in my son's life and could have finished His job a lot sooner if *I* hadn't gotten in the way. The boys were growing up and they needed, more than ever, that father-son instruction – to be dealt with as young men and not little children.

One late summer day, the principal of the Christian school called me in and told me that my younger son, Blake, would be welcome to come back for the upcoming school year, but not my older son. Deep down in my heart, I knew that the principal's decision was right, but I was so hurt. I loved my Christian school family. Our boys were only there because of God's mercy and grace. He had provided scholarships for them.

After leaving the principal's office, the boys and I walked hand in hand across the parking lot of the school. I was crying so hard that I'm sure they felt sorry for me. My heart was troubled, not only for this situation but because our family would soon be opening our first free Christian preschool to help little children receive a Christian education in one of the poorest neighborhoods in Atlanta. I just didn't need this, too.

It was then that I heard a voice say very clearly, *You can't open Christian schools for poor children – just look at your own son!* I knew it was Satan's voice and he had been given place through my son's disobedience. I was mad at Satan, I was mad at my son…and let's just say it was a bad day for me.

Later on that week, when Kells II slammed his bedroom door and stormed out of the house, I knew that he was angry at himself and at me. I thought to myself, *he is so rebellious.*

Then I heard my heart: *If you keep calling your son rebellious, that's exactly what you'll get.*

I was shocked. "Then what do You want me to call him, Lord? Just look at him."

Immediately God gave me this Scripture from the book of Ezekiel, instructing me to pray these verses over Kells II, using his name to make the Word personal. Every day after that, I began to thank God that He was replacing my son's "heart of stone" – hard, stony, rebellious – with a "heart of flesh" – pliable, teachable, moldable (36: 26, 27). I thanked Him that our son was wise and obedient, that he walked in truth and was becoming the man of God he was called to be.

God honored His Word, and when Kells II was eighteen, he got down on his knees, asked the Lord to forgive him and surrendered his life to Jesus. He started preaching and teaching at nineteen, has the voice of an angel and ministers in song, and in now president of our worldwide children's ministry.

Through that experience the Lord taught me to pray the answer and not the problem, to see with His eyes and not my own, and to call forth what is not visible as though it were. I have passed this revelation on to other parents and have seen God do great things for their children as well. Praise God for His faithfulness!

Prayer: *Heavenly Father, I am so glad that You have taken care of my boys during some hard times. Thank You for sending Your Holy Spirit to guide them and comfort them. I understand now what Your apostle John meant when he wrote, "I have no greater joy than to [know] that my children walk in truth" (3 John:4). I will be forever grateful to You for helping my sons to become the godly young men they are today. I love You, Lord. In Jesus' name, amen.*

15

Warm Hands

Except you become as little children, you cannot enter the kingdom of heaven. Whoever shall humble himself as this little child, the same is the greatest in the kingdom of heaven.

--Matthew 18: 3,4

I woke up one morning in tremendous pain from a back injury that week. On this particular day I was to meet with an editor friend, who planned to interview me about Feed My Lambs. Our meeting was scheduled to be held in one of the preschools founded by the ministry. Though I was excited to see the children, I was disappointed that I could not bend down to love on them because of my back.

"Get the children to pray for Ms. Elizabeth's back," my friend told the teachers. "She's really in pain."

As I stood there, all the three-, four- and five-year-olds surrounded me, laying their hands on my back. As the children and teachers prayed, I could feel heat coming from all those little hands. After the prayer, my back was totally healed – the heat was still there as proof. I could then bend over and hug all the children. I kissed them and I blessed them. I just loved all the little children God had brought to our free Christian preschool.

It reminded me of Matthew 21:16: "Out of the mouth of babes and nursing infants You have perfected praise."

I remember speaking at a fund-raiser once when the Lord reminded me that I, too, was one of these children.

I, too, am the child of divorced parents.

I, too, lived in government housing for a short time.

I, too, lived in mobile home parks.

I, too, had an alcoholic dad.

I, too, moved two or three times a year, traveling back and forth between my parents, living a few months with each one.

I, too, used to be one of the lambs our ministry now feeds.

If someone had not loved me, my brother and sister and I would not have learned about God's love. How awesome that He sent me back into the housing homes and impoverished neighborhoods to get the children. He has asked me to love and serve others, to preach the gospel and to open Christian schools. The seed that was sown when I was a little child is being harvested in my adult years as I have the privilege of winning souls for Jesus, Praise God!

The moment you get out of yourself and lay down your self-centeredness and pride, God will manifest His will, plan and purpose for your life through Jesus Christ and fill you with the Holy Spirit just as He did for me.

We, at Feed My Lambs, are called to be missionaries in our own back yard a well as around the world. In our schools, we teach foundational principles with a focus on academic excellence. With God's help we hope to leave a legacy of His love for generations to come.

Prayer: *I am so humbled, Lord, that You would choose me, my family and Your people to "go get the children." Thank You for trusting us to build Your schools. Thank You for giving us an opportunity to make a difference in the lives of children all over the world. Through Christ, we can do all things. I love You, Lord. In Jesus' name, amen.*

16

The Sapphire Ring

[God] is able to do exceedingly abundantly above all
that we ask or think.

--Ephesians 3:20

One year, while I was busy ministering and loving on God's
people, my husband Kells was thinking about our wedding
anniversary that was coming up. His construction work had
slowed down, and that meant there was very little money in our
account. He was doing his best to help me with the ministry as
well as taking care of the boys when I was out preaching and
singing. But my husband loved and adored me so much, he was
sad that he wouldn't be able to do anything special for me like he
had during the years when he had been making big money as a
businessman.

"Baby, I was hoping to take you out to dinner for our
anniversary," my Kells said apologetically, "but I'm afraid I can't
even do that...I'm so sorry."

"Oh, that doesn't matter," I assured him. "I have you and the
boys and God, and I don't need anything else."

I really meant that. I was so over those years when I pursued "stuff" – fine cars, houses, trips, jewelry. In fact, I had learned to trust God for every single thing we needed – and dinner at a fancy restaurant was certainly not on the list of things we *needed*.

The morning of our anniversary, I woke up to find a small box with a love letter from Kells, written on a piece of lined notebook paper. Can you imagine my surprise when I opened the box to find a beautiful sapphire and diamond ring?!

I woke my husband, kissed him and asked, "Honey, where did *this* come from?"

That's when I heard the whole story. A couple of days before, a friend of ours, Donna, had dropped by to leave a gift for me. It was the ring. She told Kells that God had laid me on her heart, and that she was just being obedient. She said she *knew* it was God because she *loved* that ring! Neither of us had said a thing to her about our anniversary.

My sweet husband was as blown away as I was. "I prayed, but..." he began, and tears welled up in his eyes. "Wow, baby! I just thought God was going to give me some extra work or something."

What Kells didn't know at that moment was that God was teaching him some of the same lessons I had learned – and some I hope you will come to know for yourself – that our Lord is kind and generous and that He loves to give good gifts to His children.

Kells had already experienced humility: He had gone from being CEO of a company to pushing a broom at Captain Billy's. But now he was learning that when we love God, when we serve Him and others, God answers our prayers in ways that are beyond anything we could ask or even imagine. Not only that, but He's always right on time.

Much later, I learned that the sapphire is the symbol of heaven and joyful devotion to God. What a sweet tribute to our marriage and ministry. God is so good!

Prayer: *Praise God! You are so awesome! Not only did I receive a beautiful ring, but also my sweet husband saw Your faithfulness when You answered beyond his heart's desire. Heavenly Father, thank You so much. You are our most beautiful blessing! I love you. In Jesus' name, amen.*

17

911

Call to Me and I will answer you, and show you
great and *mighty things, which you do not know.*

--Jeremiah 33:3

"Call 911! Mother can't breathe!"

It seemed like hours before the ambulance arrived to take my
mother to Crawford Long Hospital. Her condition was serious – a
horrible lung disease caused from smoking most of her life. Our
whole family was in tears, thinking that this would be the last
time we would see her alive.

I didn't believe God wanted my mother to die from black
lung disease – not the God I served. She was only in her sixties –
much too young to die, I thought. As the ambulance arrived at
the hospital, Mom was lifted onto a gurney and rolled into the
Intensive Care Unit. The doctors were doing all they could, but
they didn't seem very optimistic.

Every day I knelt to pray, "Lord, if You want to take my
mother Home, that's fine, but no devil in hell or sickness is going
to kill her! Show me, Lord, how to believe and stand in the gap
for my mom."

It seemed I had two choices – either believe what my eyes saw in the natural, or believe what God said about my mother's condition. After I prayed, I heard God speak Psalm 118:17 into my heart. *[Your mother] shall not die, but live, and declare the works of the Lord.* I had never seen that verse before, but I believed it!

By faith, I went into the ICU, where my mother – all ninety-seven pounds of her – was hooked up to all kinds of machines. If I had believed what my eyes saw in the natural, I would have given up right then. But I didn't care that she looked like death. I didn't care what the doctors said. I anointed her with oil and shouted: "Mother, God said you shall not die, but live, in Jesus' name! Believe that with me!" I knew in my heart that she was going to live … and she did. Praise God!

Because I sought the Lord diligently, He reached down from heaven and poured out His mercy that day. My mother and I had five more precious years together.

I don't know what you are feeling in your life right now but take a few minutes to get down on your knees with a humble heart and cry out to God. He says, "Call to Me, and I will answer you, and show you great and mighty things, which you do not know." (Jer. 33:3)

God gave us His Word and His Holy Spirit to instruct us. He wants His children to trust Him in all things, to come to Him first, to acknowledge Him and to love Him with all our hearts. How wonderful it is to trust in God and to feel free to call on Him whenever we have a need – as I did when my mother was so ill. His promise is to answer that call by showing us "great and mighty things." My mother's life, given back to me, was one of those "great and mighty things."

Remember, the world's emergency call number is 911, but God's crisis call number is Jeremiah 33:3. Only believe.

Prayer: *Father God, You were so kind and generous to give me five more years with my mother. You do answer our calls! Thank You for all the great and mighty things we learn when we trust You to answer our prayers according to Your plan and in Your time. I love you. In Jesus' name, amen.*

18

The Little Hooch

But without faith it is impossible to please [God],
because [anyone] who comes to God must believe
that He is, and that He is a rewarder of those who
diligently seek Him.

--Hebrews 11:6

In the late '80s, my husband Kells and I lived with his mom. I
was volunteering in the ministry as well as working for my brother
in the wood flooring business, and Kells worked in construction
with his brother and nephew as jobs became available.

We had received some free passes for Whitewater, a water
park in the area. One day when Kells was not working and I was
busy, he planned to go pick up some children from the government
housing homes and take them to the water park. The kids were
so excited to be going with "Mr. Kells." I would be joining them
later.

The morning Kells was leaving, we didn't have the money to
buy lunch for them at the park. "Let's pray and believe God to
provide," I told him, and we did.

Before Kells left the house, he saw some change in a jar that belonged to his brother. As he reached in to get the money, God told Kells to put it back and trust Him.

Kells drove by for the children, and they all piled into the car and headed for the water park. On the way, he prayed again that God would provide their lunch.

Their very first ride was the *Little Hooch*. You get in a tube and float around the park on a little "river." When I arrived at the park around noon, I was surprised to find out that Kells and the kids had already eaten lunch.

"Where did you get the money?" I asked. "Right after I prayed, I got in the water and a twenty-dollar bill floated up between my toes!" Kells told me. "Praise God!"

To say the least, Kells and the children had a God-given lunch to enjoy. Isn't our Lord wonderful? He loves us so much that sometimes He even goes above and beyond what we are asking.

I know it seems like a little thing, but God uses little things to teach us big lessons. Money is a sore subject with a lot of people, and He knows it can *make* or *break* relationships. In fact, money problems are at the root of many divorces, and when God is dealing with us to show us where our hearts are, He often uses financial pressure to teach us how to rely on Him. We are either living in the earthly kingdom or the Heavenly kingdom. We cannot live in both.

Jesus wants us to know that we can *step out of the boat* and onto the water – not into the water, just as His disciple Peter did. Peter started out *on* the water, but he ended up *in* the water. Why? Because he took his eyes off Jesus and began to focus on the problem (see Matt. 14:22-33).

The crashing waves of life can surely distract us from our faith-walk with Jesus, but we must continually keep our eyes on Him. How many times must we ride around in circles in the *Little Hooch* before we actually "get it"?

Let me encourage you to keep looking to the Lord Jesus

Christ as your answer and stop looking at the problem. He wants you to be amazed at His love for you.

Prayer: *Heavenly Father, I am so glad that you care for us always – during the hard times and during the times of plenty. Thank You for feeding us when we have no food, for encouraging us when we have no hope and for providing for us, over and over again, that in You all our needs are met. I love You, Lord, in Jesus' name, amen.*

19

El Eden Village

Oh, taste and see that the Lord is good; Blessed is the man who trusts in Him! Oh, fear the Lord, you His saints! There is no want to those who fear Him

--Psalm 34:8,9

One Saturday, while speaking at a women's conference in Atlanta, I shared about my life and the vision God had given me for Feed My Lambs.

Afterward, a beautiful Hispanic woman named Magda came up to me and asked, "Would you come to Mexico and help the poor children in my country?"

"I'll go wherever God opens the door," I assured her. "He has called me to help poor children by opening Christian schools all over the world."

Later on, Magda introduced my husband and me to Pastor and Mary Maranda of Piedres Negras, Mexico. On a map, they pointed out some land in a village called El Eden, which was known for its drug trafficking. Many people feared for the children's lives there.

By faith, I asked Kells to go on ahead to Piedras Negras, along with a few missionaries, and get things ready to build a school.

Kells looked puzzled. "Baby, how do you think we're going to build a school with no money?"

Before he could blink, I replied, "I don't know, but God does. Let's just go. He will provide when we get there."

Not knowing a word of Spanish and with only forty dollars in his pcket, Kells agreed to fly to Mexico, using a "buddy pass" that was given to him. I don't know which of us had the greater faith for this adventure, but we were evidently God's chosen team.

After we arrived in Mexico, I returned a call that had been forwarded to my office. The callers were a young couple from Alaska, Jordan and Jeannie, who told me that the Lord had laid on their heart the desire to give our ministry nine thousand dollars. They had no idea about our plan to build a school in Mexico...or that we were in Mexico at that very moment. Before we even left the country, our first building was built *and* paid for, praise God!

I always tell people, when God is in the plan, it will succeed. I believe that the heart of God is for every child to be brought up in a Christian environment—in schools where the gospel of Jesus Christ is shamelessly taught.

Today, what once was a drug village – El Eden in Piedras Negras, Mexico – is known as a Christian village. There are presently four school buildings (K-6), with plans for one more and a chapel to be built later. Our hope is to add high school grades in the near future. Potentially, three to four hundred children may be enrolled in this Christian school built by faith in God. All to His glory!

Together we can make a difference in the lives of children by giving them the love of Jesus and a Christian education in the U.S., Mexico and throughout the world.

Prayer: *I praise You, Lord, for opening doors for us to take Your message of love to the children of the world. Through the power and leading of Your Spirit, we have been able to do what we could never have done in our own strength. Thank You for increasing our faith. You are an awesome God, and I love you. In Jesus' name, amen.*

20

Put on a Happy face

But seek first the kingdom of God and His righteousness,
and all these things shall be added to you.

-- Matthew 6:33

One morning, when I was almost out of makeup, I mixed my foundation with water to make it stretch just one more time. Knowing that we didn't have the twenty dollars for something so unimportant, I said a little prayer: "Lord, You know I'd like some new makeup. I love You and trust You for it."

I can't remember if it was that same day or the next that my mother dropped by to see me. I hadn't told her about my predicament, so she didn't know that I needed anything. When she was leaving, I kissed her good-bye and went back into the house.

After a minute or two, I was surprised to hear her honking her horn, so I ran back out to see what she wanted.

"The Lord told me to give you this twenty-dollar bill," she yelled through the open window of the car.

"Are you sure?" I asked.

"Yes, take it!" she snapped. "God told me to do it."

I could tell from her tone of voice that she was not one bit happy about it. Only later did I learn that this was the last bill she had in her wallet. Still, I knew in my heart that God had spoken to her about blessing me. My trust was in Him, not in my mother. Obviously though, God had chosen to use her as the vessel to provide for me, reluctant as she was.

Want to know how the story ended? Before my mother's head hit the pillow that night, someone had given her *five times* that amount! God loves you and me so much that He is happy to bless us in the little things of life as well as the big things. By sharing these testimonies with you, I am hoping to encourage you to trust in God for all things and know that He will answer when the time is right.

Ever since I surrendered my life to God and began to love Him with all my heart, all my soul, all my mind and all my strength, my desires have changed. My walk, my talk, my thinking, my attitude – everything has changed. I am not saying I am perfect or totally mature in the Lord, but now, praise God, I can say I am on the right track – and I have never been happier in my life.

God told us through His Word, "Blessed [happy] is the man who trusts in Him [the Lord]" (Ps. 34:8b). Can you tell that I am so excited about my Lord? It doesn't take new makeup to make me happy in Him, but He loves me enough to provide even the small things when I trust Him. Trusting God for everything should come naturally to a born-again believer.

Through the death and resurrection of God's Son, Jesus Christ, we who believe have been brought into a relationship with our Heavenly Father. We are His children. He loves us so much that He sent His only begotten Son, who had no sin, to die for our sins. Today, Jesus is alive and we are alive in Him.

Prayer: *Thank you, Heavenly Father, for always meeting our need, however great or small. I am so grateful that no matter how young or old we may be, we can always learn more about Your goodness, mercy and love as we trust in You. I love You, Lord. In Jesus' name, amen.*

PART III
"OBEY ME"

The Lord our God we will serve,
and His voice we will obey.

--Joshua 24:24

21

"If You Love Me..."

If you love Me, keep My commandments.

--John 14:15

Love and obedience go hand in hand. As I grow in the Lord, I continue to learn what loving God means. I have come to see that obedience is an expression or fruit of my love for Him.

As you know by now, I was in my thirties before I made Jesus Lord of my life. Before that time, I loved Jesus the best I knew how. I accepted Him as my Savior in my childhood years. I enjoyed going to church, reading my Bible, praying at night and blessing my food at the dinner table. In my teenage years, I would kiss my Bible before going to sleep at night. Deep inside my heart, I loved Jesus, but as I grew older, I began to enjoy and to follow after the things of the world (see 1 John 2:15 – 17). At the same time, I would ask God to bless *my* will for my life. I was learning very well how to walk down the road of self-centeredness and deception.

Remember, as I mentioned earlier, until Christ was given Lordship over our lives, my husband and I did not have a well-balanced marriage. We both had come from families that dealt with alcohol. My family had the added history of divorce, and my husband's dad did not set a godly example in his home. Our parents loved us, but I will not pretend nor be deceived about our upbringing. I know what it is like without Jesus as Lord of the home, and I know what it is like when He is Lord of our home. There truly is a difference. In all those years of doing things our own way, we were only "one choice away" from God's best.

Unless we choose to surrender daily to Jesus, we can make a big mess of things. We don't know what is best; only God knows. Loving Him, trusting Him and obeying Him are choices we all have to make. God will never force His will on us. He desires that all we do, say or think be done because we love Him, not because we feel obligated. Love delights in giving, serving and obeying. Obedience that pleases God is never out of duty – because *I should* – but out of grateful love – because *He gave*.

Why would we not desire to please our Lord by following Him obediently? God never intended for us to be independent of Him. Never! He created us for His good pleasure and for intimate fellowship. Our obedience to the principles He has given us in His Word are all for our good and His glory…and is the evidence that we really do love Him.

I truly believe that God gave me a mandate to open Christian schools in poverty-stricken areas. It was my choice to obey or not to obey. God is going to build His kingdom with or without our help. He gives us the opportunity to share with Him the joy of kingdom-building. But if we choose not to do what He asks of us, He will raise up someone else.

Today I am so honored that God chose me, anointed me and sent me out to love others, especially the little children. Are you ready today to have a loving relationship with the Lord? If you already know and love Him, you, too, are blessed to be chosen.

Prayer: *God, You are so good. I love You so much. Thank you, Jesus, for all that You have already done for me on the cross. Help me to listen and obey each day. Teach me that obedience is for my protection and is the fruit of my love for You. In Jesus' name, amen.*

22

Let Go and Let God

I have set before you life and death, blessing and cursing; therefore choose life… that you may obey His voice, and that you may cling to Him.

--Deuteronomy 30: 19,20

Let Go I heard in my spirit one day as I was on my way downstairs to the basement of my mother-in-law's home. I was going to the fridge to take out the six-pack of beer my husband had just bought. I was furious at him for drinking, so I thought I would throw every beer can into the trash. Even though I had asked God to deliver Kells from alcohol, I just figured I'd help Him out a little.

On this particular morning, I heard in my heart a very clear word from the Lord: *Do you want Kells to quit drinking for you or for Me?*

"Spiritual giant" that I was, I immediately replied, "For *You,* Lord."

The small voice came again. *Let go.*

At that point, I obeyed. I put the beer cans back in the refrigerator and walked away. Once I yielded the whole thing to the Lord, He gave me the grace to be quiet. He told me to take my eyes off Kells and keep my eyes on Him, and He would heal our home.

My conversation with the Lord continued. "Then teach me to pray for my husband."

I want you to see Kells through My eyes.

"Well, how do You see him, Lord?"

I see him saved, healed, delivered, set free and cleansed by the blood of Jesus, My son.

"But just look at Kells! He won't go to church with me and he won't stop drinking."

From that day forward, I did not complain anymore. I obeyed God and began walking around our house, thanking Him that my husband was a mighty man of God, an overcomer. As I was faithful to pray this way, the Lord placed His unconditional love for Kells in my heart.

Would you like to know what happened when I "let go" and obeyed God? One afternoon, as Kells was driving home from work, on his way to pick up his usual six-pack, the fear of God came upon him so strongly, he knew it was the Lord.

My husband told me later that every hair on his head stood straight up! Now you have to know that Kells was use to working in the Atlanta nightclubs his dad owned, so he wasn't afraid of a good fight. But that day the fear of God came upon him so strongly, he knew it was the Lord.

When God spoke to him, he quickly replied, "I'm willing, Lord, but You're going to have to help me." After that, he quoted the only Bible verse he could think of, which was: "I'll never leave you nor forsake you" (Heb. 13:5). That was good enough for Kells.

When he got home, he began to walk through the house, getting rid of every beer can and liquor bottle he found. In one day, my strong, handsome husband was delivered from alcohol, with no more desire to drink daily.

Whatever you are going through today, I encourage you to let go of your problem, trust and obey God and watch what He does for you. Then don't forget to give God all the glory.

Prayer: *Father, I will never stop thanking You for helping my husband and me to "let go: of our own way – the way that leads to destruction. But every day there are choices. Help me always to let go and let You lead. I love You, Lord. In Jesus' name, amen.*

23

Happy Birthday, Jesus!

Inasmuch as you did it to one of the least of these My brethren, you did it to Me.

--Matthew 25:40

Kenya...November 6, 2006...God sent five of us from the ministry to Githurai Kimbo Village on the outskirts of Nairobi in Kenya, Africa. Tania, Gib, Robin, Jeremiah and I had the privilege of ministering to more than three thousand children, showing them how to celebrate the true meaning of Christmas with a "Happy Birthday, Jesus!" party. Our hosts, Pastor James Wesonga, his wife Mercy and their daughter Lydia opened up their home to us.

We first ministered to the adults, sharing God's principles on family matters. After four days, our team finished bagging three-thousand plus of gifts to give to the children at the party.

When the day arrived, the roads were muddy following an overnight downpour. Because the people had to walk from their villages to the party, the pastor wasn't sure how many would show up. We all believed that God would come through and He did! In spite of the wet and muddy roads, a big bus rolled up to drop off many of the children.

We had decided to offer a women's conference as well, and many of the women would be coming from different villages. That day more than one hundred women poured through the doors!

God led me to speak to them about loving Him first, praying for their families and thanking God for answers *before* they saw the result of their prayers. I gave my testimony about how God delivered my husband from alcohol and how I surrendered my life to Jesus and made Him Lord. I also shared about how we are to bless God daily by loving, trusting and obeying Him and that He is pleased when we love and serve others. Approximately twenty to thirty women gave their lives to Jesus for the first time, and others repented for walking away from God.

When the time came for the party, the church that holds nearly fifteen hundred people was jammed with three thousand children – two kids per chair – not including the parents, pastors and teachers. The children were well-behaved and so happy. This was the first "Happy Birthday, Jesus!" party they had ever attended. They loved the red balloons, red and green gift bags filled with toys and the big "Happy Birthday, Jesus!" cake.

After a nourishing meal, a well-known African entertainer held a mini-concert for the kids. Hundreds of children raised their hands to receive salvation. What a blessing it was to lead many of those children and their parents to Jesus.

God was so good to show us the fruits of our labor. Later that week, the pastor was told by a mother that her son came home from the party and said, "Mama, you don't have to beat me anymore with the cane. I have Jesus in my heart now, and I'll be good."

When we first arrived in Kenya, I was surprised to meet a gentleman from TBN (Trinity Broadcasting Network) who invited me to appear on their telecast. God had already opened the door for me to be on TBN many times in the past in Atlanta, Georgia, to share about our ministry, but to be in Kenya Africa?

How awesome is our God! It is amazing to see how He provides when we obey Him.

Prayer: *Lord, thank You for teaching me that obedience is the open door to Your provision. Your ways are higher than my ways. Thank You, God, for sending me and my friends to Africa for the "Happy Birthday, Jesus!" party and for opening the door to the world for Your glory. But most of all, thank You, Heavenly Father, for drawing many to You that day through Your precious Holy Spirit. I love You, Lord. In Jesus' name, amen.*

24

My Lamb's Wool Coat

*Do not despise the chastening of the Lord, nor be
discouraged when you are rebuked by Him; for whom
the Lord loves, He chastens.*

--Hebrews 12:6

After I made Jesus Lord of my life, I really began to seek the face
of God. I have told you that I went to church often and studied
the Word. In Bible college, I listened to sermons from many of
the great teachers of our day. One class, "God's Victorious Army,"
was led by a godly woman whose name was Gloria. I praise God
for her. She taught me how to be a warrior in God's Army. God
disciplined me through her during this time too. I remember the
other students feeling sorry for me after class because the Lord,
through Gloria, would correct me.

Gloria was a beautiful, six-foot-tall, African-American drill
sergeant for Jesus. The Lord knew what was ahead and He had
to do a quick work. It was boot camp for me!

You see, the more I sought God's truth, the more I understood
that discipline was a sign of His love. I was learning not to be so
self-centered and greedy and to mature in Christ.

But the Lord had much more to teach me. My car payment was due. Financially, it did not look so good. It was during this dark time that I heard the Lord telling me to give Gloria my favorite item of clothing, which was a lamb's wool coat.

What was that? I wondered. Surely I hadn't heard correctly. So I went on about my business, ignoring God's voice and His instruction.

A second time I heard Him say, *Give Gloria your lamb's wool coat.*

Again I refused. I *loved* that coat. Why would I want to give it away?

When the voice spoke to my spirit the third time – *Give Gloria the coat* – I knew in my heart that it was really God speaking to me. This time, I obeyed.

I took Gloria the coat and told her what God had lain on my heart. She knew that I had heard from the Lord. As soon as I released my coat and obeyed God, He supernaturally provided our car payment and all our needs were met. Praise God!

Did you know that when God instructs you to do something, He is just setting you up for a blessing? As soon as we take our eyes off ourselves and help others, the windows of heaven are opened over us (see Mal. 3:11). I know this for a fact. God had blessed our family so many times when we loved Him, trusted Him and obeyed Him.

I really do not think it was coincidental that (1) the coat was my favorites, and (2) it was made from lamb's wool. God always accomplishes multiple blessings when He works in us. Gloria was blessed with a beautiful coat. I was blessed by being able to keep my car.

Better than the physical blessings were the spiritual lessons I learned that day. The coat just "happened" to be made of lamb's wool. *Jesus* is the Lamb of God who was slain for our sins. By giving Gloria the coat, I was covering her with *Jesus*. And because it was my favorite coat, I was giving God my first fruits.

Prayer: *Dear Lord, You always have a greater plan for our lives than we could possibly dream for ourselves. With every blessing comes an instruction. Holy Spirit, please help us to listen and obey. What a joy it is to give. Receiving is just a bonus. I love You, Lord. In Jesus' name, amen.*

25

Another Mary

*Do not fear, little flock, for it is your Father's good
pleasure to give you the kingdom.*

--Luke 12:32

Coming home one night from the homeless women's shelter, I
was singing and praising God. The Lord had truly blessed the
women and children that night, and I was so happy to be serving
Him. I remembered telling Him, "I have decided, Lord, that I
am going to love and serve You and others. So You pick out what
I drive, where I live and even what I wear. I don't have time to do
all those things."

I meant that with all my heart and I still do. I am so honored to
tell the lost about the love of Jesus. God has blessed us abundantly
above anything we could ever ask or believe. We don't deserve all
God's blessings. We didn't earn any of them. In fact, "every good
gift and every perfect gift is from above, and comes down from
the Father of lights" (Jas 1:17). I have found that when we pray to
God and trust Him to provide for us, He is already at work. In
my case God was planning to provide through another believer,
my sweet friend Mary...

God moved on Mary's heart in a huge way once when my husband, the boys and I were actually homeless for a short season. We had been invited to stay in Bob and Marylee's big, beautiful home during this time when we got a phone call from Mary. She said that the Lord told her to give us a five-bedroom, three-bath, 3,000-square foot house. She had bought the house five weeks earlier, expecting to move in herself. But she felt she was to give it to us – no money down. We could have all the equity in it and Mary had planned to make the house payments for two years in advance. Our family could hardly believe it! Praise God! We were so excited, so thankful to Him!

On the day that we moved in, there was new white carpet throughout. At that time we had only a king-sized bed that was donated to us, a queen-sized bedroom suite that a furniture store had given to us earlier and a buffet we had bought when our youngest son Blake was born. But God knew what we needed. I would just be patient and trust Him.

Two or three weeks later, my precious friend Donna called. "I'm moving out of my townhouse and going into full-time ministry," she said. "Would you like to have my furniture?"

Talk about timing! There were two white sofas, a cherry dining room suite, silk flowers, lamps, tables and picture. I shouted! I danced! I praised God! Within a month, our family who loved God, who trusted God, who obeyed God, had a new home and new furniture. Since 1989, God has used Mary to provide many vehicles for our family – cars, trucks, vans, and even the beautiful white BMW I am driving today. God is faithful.

I'm not saying that God is going to give everyone who reads this book a new home, but I do want you to understand that when we choose to love, trust and obey Him, He promises to add all things to us. As we love and serve, we can rest and not stress about our daily needs.

And what about the one who obeys God by giving? I think of the Mary's of the Bible: Mary, the mother of Jesus, who obeyed

God and gave her body to carry the Holy Child. Mary Magdalene, who gave her Lord adoration and devotion. Mary, the sister of Martha, who gave Jesus her undivided attention and sat at His feet, drinking in every word. And then there is our Mary, who has given so much love to me and my family and has contributed to God's ministry for nearly 31 years. She will tell you that her obedience has brought greater blessings than she could ever have imagined.

Maybe there is a time when you are to give rather than receive. How will you know? Ask the Lord, "How can I bless You?" When He shows you, be quick to obey. We can never lose when we give in love.

Prayer: *Dear Lord, You know someone who needs me. Please tell me how I can bless You and others today. You have so faithfully cared for me and my family all these years, and now my greatest joy, just like the Mary's of the Bible and our own Mary, is to give back as You have given to me. I love you, Lord. In Jesus' name, I pray, amen.*

26

Choose Life

I have set before you life and death, blessing and cursing; therefore choose life.

--Deuteronomy 30:19

Before I was born again, I had some unhealthy habits. I ate chips, drank Cokes and baked myself in the sun for hours. I guess you could say I was a little self-centered.

Things did change after I made Jesus Lord of my life. I was so happy, I just could not get enough of God's Word. I prayed a lot. When I went to Bible college I began to gain understanding of His wisdom in making decisions for my life – from taking better care of my physical health to nourishing my soul. My beliefs about God were strengthened as I hungered for His truth.

Deciding to become spiritually healthy is a choice that begins in the mind, knowing the truth and then acting on it. The Bible says: "My people are destroyed for lack of knowledge. Because you have rejected knowledge, I also will reject you from being priest for Me; because you have forgotten the law of your God, I also will forget your children" (Hos. 4:6) I believe that what God is saying to us today is that sometimes we are physically and mentally sick because we are spiritually sick. Why do I say that? Because God tells us in Pslam 107:20: "He sent His word and healed them."

Gradually, as I surrendered more and more to the leading of the Holy Spirit, I began to put others before myself. My heart changed. My health habits changed. My mindset changed. My attitude changed. My conversation changed. Praise God! My new life in Jesus Christ and my love for Him is exciting. It has affected every part of me!

Do I have days of discouragement? Yes. Do I still mess up? Yes. Do I blow it as a Christian? Yes. But when I do, I acknowledge my sin, repent and ask for forgiveness. I know Jesus forgives me (see 1 John 1:9) and the Holy Spirit in me is guiding me and enabling me to walk in truth and forgiveness (see John 16:13).

Just like a baby learning to walk, we sometimes stumble. Our Father is right there to catch us when we fall and His Spirit is always there to guide and sustain us.

Obedience is often given a bad rap. We think it is the end of our freedom when actually it is the beginning. The word *obey* literally means "to open the door." That means we haven't even begun to live in the blessings God has for us and for others until we walk through that door of obedience.

I have been on this journey for almost thirty-five years and the Lord has never failed me. While you and I are still on this earth, we are given choices every day. Let's choose the activities, the food, the lifestyle, the mate, the friendships that will enrich our lives. Let's choose Jesus, who is "the way, the truth, and the life" (John 14:6).

Prayer: *Dear Lord, I love You. I need You in my life to guide and direct my steps. Help me to always obey You. My heart wants to do what is right – to be a blessing to You always and forever. In Jesus' name, amen.*

27

More Than Enough

Cursed is the man who trusts in man and makes flesh
his strength, whose heart departs from the Lord.

Blessed is the man who trust in the Lord, and whose
hope is the Lord.

--Jeremiah 17: 5,7

"What's going on here, Libby? There's practically nothing in your pantry!"

On a visit to our home one day, my mother happened to open our pantry door and discovered that it was almost bare. Of course, I wasn't the least bit worried. I had just begun volunteering in the ministry, so we only had one income. But Kells and I knew that God had called me and He would provide for our family. However He chose to provide was fine with me.

"Oh, it's going to be okay, Mother," I replied. "Kells just hasn't been paid yet."

I thought of the time when Moses was leading God's people through the wilderness. They were murmuring and complaining because they were hungry and thirsty. Well, I certainly didn't intend to act like that! I knew that if God could bring water from a rock and send manna from heaven, He could do the same for me and my family. My God is true to His promises, and He has promised to take care of His children. That's why I hadn't bothered to share our need with anyone – not even with my mother.

When I first went into fulltime ministry, the Lord put a Scripture in my heart – Jeremiah 17: 5, 7. Here the Lord speaks about trusting in Him and not in people. I knew I was to obey... or else.

Would you believe that by the end of the day, my mother had told my only brother, Robert, about our situation- that we had no groceries in the house and that my husband had not been paid? My precious brother felt he was directed by God to take action. Our entire family was blessed that day because of his obedience by his gift of $500.

What he gave us was more than enough. One day, no food. The next day, an overflowing pantry. So much food, in fact, that we were able to share with some neighbors who were also going through hard times. My precious brother recognized the voice of God and obeyed it, and our entire family was blessed that day.

Right after Robert obeyed God, his flooring business began to prosper in a mighty way. He knew it was God who had blessed him abundantly. All of a sudden, retail stores were calling on him as well as Georgia Tech and the University of Georgia. I am also happy to say that my brother has made Jesus Christ his Lord. Our God is an awesome God!

How many times does God give us opportunities to be a blessing to others and we either don't hear Him or we don't listen and obey? When we fail to do that, we miss our very own blessing. The Lord clearly said to me recently, "Stay focused on obedience to Me and not on money, and all other things shall be added."

Prayer: *Heavenly Father, You continue to amaze me! When You give your blessings, no one is left out. The receiver is blessed and the giver is blessed. What an awesome God we serve. Thank You for Your divine multiplication in each of our lives. I love You, Lord. In Jesus' name, amen.*

28

Blake's Story

When the enemy comes in like a flood, the Spirit of the Lord will lift up a standard against him.

--Isaiah 59:15

"Mom, I know why you talk about Jesus all the time. He's your best friend, isn't He? You hang out with Jesus, don't you, Mom?"

Blake was right. I really do hang out with Jesus. He is such a faithful friend, and He tells me things I should know ahead of time...like the night Blake and some buddies were away on an overnight camping trip.

I woke up sometime after midnight, feeling strongly that I should pray for him. I was sitting at our kitchen table with my Bible when my husband walked in from our bedroom.

"What's going on?" Kells asked. "What are you doing up at this hour of the night?"

"I don't really know," I told him, "but I just feel led to pray for Blake."

Kells sat down at the table with me and I opened the Bible to Psalm 91, one of David's songs of protection. As we prayed together for our son, those wonderful thoughts from God's Word brought so much peace to our hearts.

Since I couldn't sleep, I stayed up the rest of the night, praying and reading my Bible. Around five or six in the morning, I heard the front door open. It was Blake.

"What are you doing home so early?" I asked him.

When he told me what had happened, all I could do was cry and praise God!

"The guys and I set up our sleeping bags underneath the bridge at Little River. Then, later in the night, we decided to move our stuff to another place," he said. Then his eyes got wider. "Mom, you aren't going to believe this...a truck ran off the road and slammed into the very sport where we would have been sleeping!"

I got up and hugged Blake and told him that God woke his dad and me to pray for him and the guys. God is so good! God is so faithful! I was so thankful that Kells and I had obeyed God's prompting to pray. I believe with all my heart that God protected Blake and the other boys that night. Satan had a plan to destroy them, but God intervened in His love, grace and mercy.

Friends, you and I must continually be listening for God's still, small voice. He is speaking to us every day. But are we really listening? As He says to the churches in the book of Revelation: "He who has an ear to hear, let him hear" (2:7)

I believe that my son is alive today because his dad and I heard God's voice to pray for his safety that night...and we obeyed. Today Blake is healthy, handsome and serving in the ministry. He is a singer, songwriter and the best guitar player ever. Not only that, but he is married to a beautiful young woman named Shannon whom I love and adore.

With all the noise and commotion of this world and all the voices clamoring for our attention, it is more and more important that we hear God's voice. Expect to hear from Him, and when

He stirs in your heart, do whatever He tells you to do. It could possibly save the life of someone you love!

Prayer: *Thank You, Lord, for protecting Blake and his friends. I love You! I praise you! I am so grateful that You woke his dad and me to pray for them and proclaim Psalm 91 over them. I was so glad to see our son walk in the door of our home. Lord, Thank You for waking all of us up to hear and obey Your voice when You speak to us. You are so faithful! In Jesus' dear name, amen.*

29

That "Old-Time Religion"

To obey is better than sacrifice.

-- 1 Samuel 15:22

It's time for a heart-to-heart about religion and relationship, so listen up...

Religion is the practice of certain beliefs and rituals of faith. There are many religions: Buddhist, Muslim, Hindu, Jewish, etc. Religion is simply following a set of rules. God does not want us to be *religious*. He wants *relationship* with us.

Did you hear that? The Creator of the universe desires a relationship with you and me! Other religions are based on performance – how well we measure up to certain standards – but not Christianity. That is why I call it GOOD NEWS!

Where we get off track is that we believe God is pleased when we obey a bunch of rules. Well, I did *this* right and *this* right, but I did *this* wrong. Did I pass the test or did I fail? Am I going to heaven, or did I miss the mark somewhere? Will I have to spend eternity in hell? These are real questions that people have struggled with since the beginning of time.

It is much easier to measure our performance with God than

to have a vulnerable relationship one-on-one with Him. Satan uses this as "the great distraction" for Christians. *Just give me a good grade, Lord, and I will try to do better next time...*

No! Our 'righteousness" is like dirty rags to God (see Isa. 64:6) All He asks of us is obedience to His will for our lives. Obeying is the same as listening and doing what He says. This should be as natural for Christians as breathing is to a baby. As His children, we must believe that He wants what is best for us and that we can trust Him completely.

Remember to seek God and His righteousness first. Delight in the Lord! Praise Him. Sing to Him! Thank Him! God created us for worship and relationship. Enjoy Him!

If you will start loving on God and being obedient to His voice, you will never question your salvation again. You will never wonder if you "missed the mark." Of course, you did miss the mark. I did too. But when you accepted Jesus, you acknowledged that He took your place for sin, was crucified, died, and rose again on the third day to give you eternal life. Jesus took your sin, your sickness, your failure and gave you the privilege of living with Him for all eternity!

No one on this earth has ever done that for you except Jesus Christ, the Son of the Living God. Why would you not jump at the chance to please Him, to obey Him, to love Him? He knew you before you were born, while you were still in your mother's womb (see Jer. 1:5). He knows what you need before you even ask. What amazing love!

Friends, we must wake up, grow up and allow God, through Jesus Christ and the Holy Spirit to fill us and baptize us with His power and presence in these earthly vessels so that the world can see and know the love of Almighty God.

Let's shed the "old-time religion" that keeps us from developing a living, growing relationship with our Lord. Since my husband Kells went to be with Jesus, I made a decision to get in my Heavenly Father's lap and let Him love on me. Now *that's* a relationship!

Prayer: *Heavenly Father, help us to let go of our own "righteousness" and come to You as little children. Fill us with Your Spirit and then send us out to share Your love with others. We cannot do it without You. In Jesus' name, amen.*

30

"Come Away, My Beloved"

Rise up, My darling! Come away with Me, My fair one!

--Song of Solomon 2:10 (NLT)

I was in my bedroom reading my Bible one day when the Lord spoke to me: *I want you to hold a three-day women's retreat in the mountains of North Georgia. Call it: "Come Away, My Beloved."*

This was a first for me. I had never tried to organize a retreat before, so I didn't know anything about it. But God did.

Step one would be setting the date and time. The Lord clearly told me: *Plan the retreat for the beginning of the week.*

Faith-filled woman of God that I was, I began to argue with Him. "But, Lord, nobody will come at the beginning of the week! You know that most retreats are on the weekend."

He didn't budge an inch. *Do you want Me to fit into your schedule, Elizabeth.* He asked in that gentle voice I had come to know so well, *or do you want to fit into Mine?*

"Yours, Lord," I agreed meekly, realizing that my plans would not amount to anything if I insisted on having my own way. Not leaning on my own understanding, I asked the Lord whom I should invite. When He told me, I realized that everyone on His guest list was busy – businesswomen, moms of young children, teachers. Although none of this made any sense to me, the whole thing was not a suggestion, but a mandate, and I intended to obey every direction He gave me.

In preparation for the event, God called me to a seven-day fast. During that week, I felt led to ask my husband to build a big wooden cross. The ladies would bring pictures of their loved ones, lay them around the cross and we would pray over our families.

As the days went by, I had more questions for the Lord. "Who's going to help me do all this?" I asked. At that moment, a name popped into my mind. *Barbara*. I hadn't heard from her in ages, but I really wasn't surprised when she called me soon after that, telling me that the Lord had laid me on her heart. God continued to provide miraculously for the retreat as the day approached.

The women who came that day were responding to God's invitation to come away with Him. We fasted on the first day. There was no agenda – no preaching, no teaching, no big-screen media presentation. We just sat at Jesus' feet, praising and worshipping Him together, thanking Him for what He had already done for us and praying over the pictures we had laid at the foot of the cross.

Not only had God invited us to sit at His feet, but He had given us the opportunity to bring our families to Him as well. As we lay prostrate on the floor, with the cross in the center, we were acknowledging that we were surrendering our families to the Lord. The Spirit of God was so heavy on all of us it was as if Jesus Himself had stepped into the room. We began to weep as we realized that He was honoring us with His Presence because we so wanted to love, trust and obey Him.

All of us left the North Georgia Mountains, refreshed and strengthened, knowing that we had pleased the Lord by spending time with Him. Beloved, when the Lord invites you to come away with Him, don't miss His still, small voice. If you will obey

God and set aside your own plans to make time for Him, He will manifest Himself to you.

Prayer: *Heavenly Father, I pray that more and more of Your children will receive the invitation to come into Your Presence. Help us to overcome the distractions of our busy lives and take the time to answer when You call. May we never miss the blessings of intimate fellowship with You and all that You long to give those who love you. In Jesus' name, amen.*

31

Yes, Lord, I'll Do It!

*If you diligently obey the voice of the Lord, Your God,
to observe carefully all His commandments which I
command you today, that the Lord your God will
set you high above all nations of the earth. And all
these blessings shall come upon you and overtake you,
because you obey the Voice of the Lord.*

-- Deuteronomy 28:1,2

There came a time in my life when I had to make a decision
whether to believe that God is who He says He is...or not.
Suddenly on March 15, 2004, at age 52, two brain tumors burst
in my husband Kell's head. Later we found out that he had five
tumors. In reality, Kells should have died right then, but praise
God, He had other plans for my sweet husband. For the next year,
after three brain surgeries, Kells could see, hear, talk and even
walk. During that time, my sons, family, friends and I were right
by his side, loving and serving him every day.

Near the end of that year, when I was really exhausted, my
longtime friend Donna saw that I needed a weekend away just
to be ministered to, to be strengthened physically and spiritually

for this journey I was on. She offered to take me to a women's conference in Pensacola, Florida. Some people might have thought I should have stayed with my husband, who needed me.

But not Kells. My sweet husband, who always thought of me and the boys first, was so excited for me. "You go and get some rest, baby. I'll be just fine. Here's $80 to take with you on the trip. It's all I can give you."

I kissed him good-bye and left with Donna, who was blessing me with this gift-of-love weekend. I never will forget that morning at the service. The Holy Spirit was so strong that I was weeping. It had seemed that my life was filled with such heartache and woundedness. As I was standing there, enjoying the Presence of God with my hands stretched toward heaven, I thanked the Lord for loving me. I also asked God to strengthen and heal our family.

At that very moment, I heard clearly in my heart, *Sow $8,000 into this ministry.*

I knew my Lord's voice, so I said to Him, "You mean $80, don't You? That's all I have."

Then I heard God's voice again. *Sow $8,000.*

Immediately, I got it. "Oh, You must mean $800. I'll give $80 today toward the $800."

You have to understand that my Heavenly Father and I are having this conversation back and forth while His anointing and Presence are filling this big auditorium where thousands of people are weeping and worshipping God. But we serve a very personal God and Savior, who loves each of us individually.

Again I heard, *Give $8,000.*

I didn't know what to do, so I told the Lord, "Well, I don't have $8,000, but… yes. Lord, I'll do it! I will trust You for the money." I truly meant that. Jesus is my Lord. I desire to obey my God because I love and trust Him.

The next thing I heard was, *Now I'll do the rest. I just set you up for a blessing.*

I knew then that all God wanted from me was my obedience.

When I got home and told Kells what had happened, he grabbed both my hands and prayed, "Lord, if You want my precious wife to give this $8,000, then we trust You to provide."

I began saying to God, "Lord, show me what You want me to do, and I'll do it."

His still, small voice came again in my heart, *When you go minister and sing in churches, I want you to sow your love offering into this ministry.*

Right away God began opening doors for me to minister in many places. It was so exciting to see what God was doing as I surrendered in obedience to Him. I received the largest love offerings ever in my twenty years of ministry! Over a period of time the Lord provided the entire $8,000 to that ministry. I have learned that when God has a mandate for you and you surrender to Him and obey, He will "do the rest". God is so faithful.

The Lord is doing new things in my life now that my sweet husband is in heaven, healthy and strong. Both Kells and Blake are anointed by God in music, singing, writing. I have 2 beautiful daughters-in-love and 7 beautiful grandchildren. I confess over them that they are God's warriors in the making. I have wonderful friends and partners, and I can't wait to see what will come next for all of us.

My heart's desire for you, my new and dear friends in Christ, is that you, too, will wake up every day, asking, "Lord, how can I bless You today and be a blessing to others?" In writing this book, sharing the journey of my life, teachings from God's Word and heartfelt prayers, my hope is that you and my Lord have been blessed.

Prayer: *Heavenly Father, I love You, Lord. I worship You. I praise You and I thank You. You are an awesome Father, a loving Husband,*

Healer, Provider and Protector. You have never left me or failed me. You care for me and allow me always to come into Your loving arms. Your Presence and anointing have kept me through this journey. I love You, Lord. In Jesus' name, amen.

Covenant Prayer

Here at the end of this part of my journey, I want you to know that I already feel a connection with you. If you have come this far with me, we are friends! Know that I have been and will continue to be praying for you. God has great and wonderful things as you walk with Him.

If you feel a little distant from Him or if you have somehow wandered off the path, you're not alone. Others also need a fresh, new relationship with Jesus, so this is my heartfelt prayer for you, my precious friend. If you like, you can pray with me:

Prayer:

Dear Heavenly Father, You already know my name and my need.
You know my struggles, my failures,
My heartaches, my desires and my dreams.
Please bring me back to my First Love,
when you were all I needed.
Help me to love You with all my heart,
all my soul, all my mind,
and all my strength,
and to love my neighbor as myself.
Teach me to pray,
"Lord, how can I bless You?"
Then show me how to walk with You
more closely every day.
In Jesus' name, I pray, amen.

NOTES

_____

_____

_____

_____

_____

_____

_____

_____

_____

_____

_____

_____

_____

_____

About the Author

Elizabeth Weatherby shares her life testimony of how God called a housewife/mom/country singer to found a ministry called Feed My Lambs, a grassroots international ministry that opened tuition-free Christian schools for children in impoverished areas of the United States, Mexico and Africa. During this time Elizabeth ministered in prisons, youth detention and drug rehab centers, as well as to homeless women and children in the inner city of Atlanta, Georgia.

Elizabeth is called to "go get the babies," to teach families how to pray God's Word in faith, not wavering from His promises. She ministers hope and has God's heart to share His faithfulness to hurting families with failing marriages, rebellious teens, physical illness and financial problems. She has lived every word she teaches!

Many churches, radio stations and newspapers have recognized her outstanding community service. She was awarded the Community Service Award in 1994 by Miss Georgia USA, was chosen as the TBS Citizen of the Week in 1995, and was nominated for the 1996 Jack Vaughn Humanitarian Award for her work in the Cobb County Georgia community and she recently received an honorary doctorate from the University of Leadership and Sound Doctrine in Texas. Elizabeth and the ministry are often featured on Atlanta TV stations, TBN and WATC Channel 57, spreading the word about Jesus Christ while opening Christian preschools for homeless children in cities throughout the country. She resides in Atlanta, Georgia.

About Elizabeth Ann Ministries

We are a 501(c)3 faith-based ministry, which is supported by businesses, churches, foundations and individuals who partner with us and volunteer their time. We believe that this ministry is bringing God's people together from all denominations to serve with one heart. Together we are helping to break the cycle of poverty one child at a time.

Elizabeth ministers the gospel of Jesus Christ wherever she goes. God has called her to "go get the babies and little children for He is raising up a holy people". Together we can change a nation through Jesus Christ.

The Mission of Elizabeth Ann Ministries is to open Christian schools in poverty areas. As we follow Matthew 25: 35 and 36, we also reach out to the lost and hurting (feed the hungry, cloth the naked, visit those in prison).